FRENEMY ENABLER

How the "Loving" Create Disaster
by Who They Favor

Karen Kellock Ph.D.

Manual for Superior Men

This is a complete theory based on Einstein physics, Political Psychology, Systems Theory and Archetypal Psychiatry.

FORMULA

All success attraction
All disease obstruction
All recovery elimination

You must fast on all three

OBSTRUCTIONS:

People
Habit
Food

FRENEMY ENABLER

Queen consciousness is so twisted by the world she's struggling for affirmation like a little girl. It's scary living with your worst enemy under the same roof while he was so nice before the booze.   Those who let this stress push em away from God will have a deathbed of regrets as things go on.   You're far more attractive to a man/potential mate if deep into your own thing, never to cling.   Men sick of shallow/silly women easily hypnotized in their homes want grand dames alone.

FRENEMY

LOVE OF BEAUTY SULLIED
LEFT WITH STARTLE REFLEX
EFFECTS OF MENTAL ABUSE
LEAVING THE NARCISSIST
YOU'RE NOT ALLOWED TO LEAVE
HIS MIND IS MADE UP
LET HIM THINK HE'S WINNING
HE'LL BREAK YOU LATER TOO
HE CYCLES THRU OTHER PEOPLE
SEEKING FAME FOR SUPPLY

FRENEMY

LOVE OF BEAUTY SULLIED

I'm turned on by what I see: it inspires me. But not in a state of emergency, I was blind to beauty.

Liberalism is a mental illness and destroys the lives of any victim in their cobweb of narratives.

People: They come and go, they aren't that important and those who think they are aren't.

I shudder looking back when under the control of dumber people. Cruelty's implied, and evil.

Wisdom comes from God and those who don't have it, well forget it. I pray you escape the traps.

If those girls are giving over to you they're such fools but you already know that don't ya dudes.

LEFT WITH STARTLE REFLEX

My low startle reflex came from always being on alert in that system of domination without respect.

Having been gaslit for years with perception interfering the victim needs approval even revering.

Having looks degraded is a major trauma for now when the victim is flattered they never believe ya.

The victim over-thanks for anything/everything and can't make decisions after a system of treachery.

Victims over-thank for anything/everything and can't make decisions after the system of treachery.

FRENEMY

I was teased, taunted, humiliated and degraded: my season of treason was a sad state, ill fated.

Humiliated, degraded and insulted a million times thru many years: a history of nothing but tears.

They start to insult when you don't live up to their ideal, a utopian notion that ultimately kills/steals.

They enable you to SIN but not to overcome and expand into your potential as a champion.

They drag you down by hanging out, stopping by or just interrupting your plans for that day.

EFFECTS OF MENTAL ABUSE

The mentally abused person has a low frustration point and can react with rage/getting out of joint.

After living that way for decades the victim LIVES in fight-flight survival mode and treachery.

In this state one can't access the logical part of the brain: it's just jungle mentality/rugged terrain.

Everything is out of proportion with the mentally abused and I'd include in this the falsely accused.

To be constantly on guard and ready to defend yourself becomes the customary behavior in hell.

LEAVING THE NARCISSIST

He believed he wrecked my self-esteem so much I wouldn't be able to leave/he was shocked.

He believed his badgering me to death would prevent my permanent elimination of this threat.

FRENEMY

Narcissists live in alternate reality having created a false image/narrative of their importance see.

He saw his abusive behaviors as entitlements deserved against me and I broke through his reality.

YOU'RE NOT ALLOWED TO LEAVE

Who in hell did I think I was, leaving him? I didn't have the authority thought this mentally ill man.

Narcs are always running a phony narrative in their minds that puts em as hero, martyr or victim.

They will never accept the role of villain or abuser [no, never]--you'll have to write this off forever.

The "victim" was really the destroyer of happiness and joy. He was a bully whose goal was to annoy.

Maintaining their phony self image is foremost and if what you say contradicts that, you're toast.

The mere suggestion of the role they've played brings extreme offense so protect your pets.

HIS MIND IS MADE UP

In his mind I was beneath him, worthless compared to him. He framed me that way/I was chagrined.

Brace yourself: he's about to remind you of who runs the show and who doesn't in this hell.

Brace yourself for rage and extreme delusional thinking, all because for peace you put up with things.

Let the past go so ALL mental energy's focused on the now. It's the right-brain/a cornucopia/a miracle.

FRENEMY

it happened back then when you were both younger, now you've both aged and it's a new specter.

Stay away from people & be as independent as you can. Give em an inch and they take over man.

Disentrenching from sick systems feels like amputation but its freedom so get thru this little bit son.

Brace to be devalued, degraded and marginalized whether in court or with friends disguised.

You leave without permission and his destruction on your life is unending: good luck honey.

If you're with a high end narcissist [psychopath] try to make him leave you first or die cursed.

LET HIM THINK HE'S WINNING

Nothing's more important to him than winning so make him feel victorious as you leave him.

The narcissist I knew is dead now but I still shudder thinking of him: wow. Trapped, saved by God.

This horrible era with a narcissist will give you wisdom sis. Now find a nice man for total happiness.

The devastation he had on the body, always on the alert for his characteristic kind of hurt.

HE'LL BREAK YOU LATER TOO

He'll break you after you leave him. He's not gonna let you go on ahead and do much better friend.

He's got an attachment disorder: doesn't attach in a healthy way but also doesn't LEAVE easily.

FRENEMY

He sees you as an extension of him, he owns you. Even after relationship ends it's a problem Sue.

He doesn't want you to move forward, forget about him and have a new life with a loving man.

He wants you available to come back to whenever, so any new guy is a threat to this scammer.

In the meantime he cycles thru other women available for he always maintains a loving stable.

It's this person, then that person, they circling back. This was your reality in dark days long past.

Isn't it wonderful in your own life, not thinking about Mary, Sue or all the other girls he knew?

He sees your "moving on" as replacing HIM. Though he has no love he can't stand that my friend.

HE CYCLES THRU OTHER PEOPLE

He cycles thru other people while you're sitting home in your own little world, free of worldly evils.

Compare this to a loving husband and emotional stability so your mind and talents can expand.

Before you marry make sure you both want the same level of privacy or it'll be miserable surely.

They don't want you but you're still their property? Imagine thinking that--move on quickly.

The hoover is never about rekindling the relationship but about continuing to get SUPPLY/that's it.

SEEKING FAME FOR SUPPLY

FRENEMY

The focus and attention he got from you all along: he wants to know he can still get that hon'.

The more people he has the better for him since it's all about approval supply/he'd love to have millions.

When a child has no self-awareness or parental validation they look for it in others son.

Their attachment is ambivalent and nonbonding. It keeps you crazy not knowing what's happening.

FRENEMY ENABLER

How the "Loving" Create Disaster
by Who They Favor

CONTRADICTORY SOCIAL SIGNALS
STRESS CAN BE GOOD IF
SHALLOW VS. DEEP WOMEN
MAKE YOURSELF CRAZY TO ADAPT
HOMESICK FOR WHAT YOU NEVER HAD
SOMEHOW HER SHIP WILL COME IN
THE POWER OF SEX AND OLDER WOMEN
OLDER WOMEN AND GIGOLOS
HAPPY FAMILY MYTHOLOGY
THEY HAVE NO ANCHOR
SIBLING HATRED
SISTERS START RUMORS
HEAR THEIR TAUNTING VOICE THRU LIFE
TRUST FUND TRAGEDIES
NOSEY AND GOSSIPPY
NO RESTRAINT IN POWER PAYBACKS
I WAS MUTED BY IT BUT NOW IT'S COME OUT
IT'S THE *REPEATED* TRAUMA
TRAUMA OF CALUMNY: GETTING EM AGAINST ME
WHEN DID I LOSE MY UNIQUENESS
PEOPLE WILL ALWAYS DISAPPOINT
INSANE SOCIAL EXPECTATIONS
LOST SPIRIT ADAPTING TO DISRESPECT
SHIFTING SANDS OF DYSFUNCTION
COMPLEX PTSD BRINGS MEMORY INTRUSION
SO WEAKENED I SUCCUMBED
HORRORS: LIVING WITH SATANIC ADDICTION
EVIL SISTERS AND CINDERELLA
HAVING AGREED TO GRASSHOPPER STATUS
EVIL STEPMOTHER SYNDROME

FRENEMY ENABLER

How the "Loving" Create Disaster
by Who They Favor

SEX USED AS A BATTERING RAM AGAINST WEST
WE'RE ALL GOD: HOW SILLY THIS SAYING
DENIAL OF BINARIES IS PURE B.S.
SICKEST AND MOST PERVERTED GENERATION
PEOPLE MOURN WHEN THE WICKED RULE
HIPPYISM HIT GLITCHES AND BECAME WITCHES
GLOAL BARRACKS OR A RIGHT TO BE DIFFERENT?
ENTRY POINTS FOR DEMONS: WARNING
THE TRUTH IS STRANGER THAN FICTION
PURITANISM A REACTION TO DEBAUCHERY
POSTMODERNISM IS FAMILY FRANKENSTEIN
THE GREAT DETERMINER DECIDES FATE OF NATIONS
LIBERALISM IS A MENTAL/SPIRITUAL DISORDER
APPEASEMENT EMBOLDENS AGGRESSORS
DESPERATE NEED FOR APPROVAL
UPSIDE DOWN WORLD OF OPPOSITES
DEMS: POWER IN CITIES/WIPE OUT FARMING COMMUNITIES
THE LEFT ARE MEGALOMANIACAL
CONTINUOUS LYING OF FAKE NEWS ALL DAY
THE MORE TYRANNICAL THE QUICKER WE WAKE UP
GOOD LEADERS HATE UNJUST GAIN
OBAMANOIDS MORE DANGEROUS THAN GANGSTERS
WEAK LEADERS CREATE DISASTER
FLAWED ARGUMENTS NEED BIG GOVERNMENT
LANDSLIDES CAN'T BE STOLEN BUT THEY TOOK THE REST OF EM
OBAMA WAS DAILY TRAUMA
THE MAINSTREAM IS FAKE NEWS: SEEK TRUTH
LIBERALISM: OPEN BORDERS TO FOES
FOX MAKES DISTINCTIONS WITHOUT DIFFERENCES
AMERICA IS LIBERTY PRINCIPALS: HARDLY EVIL!
DEMOCRATS LOVE HOLLYWOOD ELITES

FRENEMY ENABLER

CONTRADICTORY SOCIAL SIGNALS

They've heard terrible stuff about you but upon meeting you're the opposite--who's the fool?

The biggest reaction of the wife of the alcoholic is to get drunk herself then she's blamed for it all.

There's a big difference between manipulating you and trying to make amends for damage done.

She's addictively tied to the toxic apologies: the same speech to a broken consciousness queen.

Queen consciousness is so twisted by the world she's struggling for affirmation like a little girl.

She thinks he's her last shot cuz he told her that: "ain't nobody gonna want you" like it's a fact.

She's forgotten that part, where he scares her with her age like she's now inferior to "her day".

Her aging is the biggest weapon he brandishes. She's over the hill, useless and it's obvious.

STRESS CAN BE GOOD IF

Eventually the stress he causes gets her back to God. Don't regret that pain if it goads you on.

Those who let his stress push em away from God will have a deathbed of regrets as things go on.

Just like shame changes behavior towards God, it's the same thing after he bashed you so loud.

FRENEMY ENABLER

Trying to heal & repair the damage they did is not manipulation so try going along with em.

It's scary living with your worst enemy under the same roof while he was so nice before the booze.

Do you know one who can't let go due to memories or "he reached out for me today" apologies?

"I saw him and he had a gleam in his eye, I know we're getting back together" and whatever.

It's hard to but DO put the energy/focus back on you. You stand alone, perfect, then a mate too.

SHALLOW VS. DEEP WOMEN

You're far more attractive to a man/potential mate if deep into your own thing, never to cling.

Men sick of shallow/silly women easily hypnotized in their homes, they want grand dames alone.

You'll believe anything, that's what he's thinking. I remember the mixed signals so sickening.

Nothing more addictive than love and you got this dude who's a clown and a loser under the rug.

Stop this, stop this now. Everyone has a talent even a rare genius inside and that's how you rule.

I remember my moods being totally dependent on the ground--my ups and downs with him around.

Why can't the poor woman let him go? Irrational hope is the devil's process to keep her roped.

She's hoping and hoping it all works out to be the dream she's had since the beginning, all cuza him.

FRENEMY ENABLER

They slurred my good name and smeared my rep. Sibling abuse can occur until we're dead.

When we moved from California to Utah people were far nicer but then again we're all sinners.

MAKE YOURSELF CRAZY TO ADAPT

Make yourself crazy to adapt to the crazy environment--how else can you do it? It's all I knew, heck.

A Christian walk can be very heavy as you start to divide from family cuz Jesus brought a sword see.

Ok so the pills you took made you crazy and lascivious. They'll still blame you for this, be sure of it.

If you see the same pattern two or three times that's who the person is/you can't change him.

I don't care how much you love them: sometimes your heart must break for your soul to heal son.

You gotta let it go: release yourself from irrational hopes which means you finally growing up.

You can't change someone who God has not changed, their momma or legal system couldn't ok.

HOMESICK FOR WHAT YOU NEVER HAD

We are homesick most for the places we've never known. What you want you've never had.

You've never experienced what you want so much cuz it "ain't in em"--it's all fantasy about a dunce.

Hope deferred makes the heart sick. You keep wishin' and hopin'/it's not happenin' = unrealistic.

FRENEMY ENABLER

Constantly being put off breaks you from the inside out. Wait for momma but she never comes: ouch.

If he hasn't changed for you, you ain't the woman he's gonna change for. Relocate or get support.

Would you keep investing in the same company when it's never made a profit/you lost everything?

SOMEHOW HER SHIP WILL COME IN

Somehow your ship is gonna finally come in and he's gonna be the man of your dreams, amen!

Why can't she just let it go? She's sexually entangled and her mind is blown from head to toes.

He ain't worth a nickel but he makes her respond in full and that's why she stays--face it girl.

Many women are addicted to the sexual pleasure an illicit man provides despite all his many lies.

"I'm outa here" she says but when the sexual soul tie kicks in and she longs for her fix that's it.

"I'm going no contact" and it lasts half a day cuz she has a sexual soul tie keeping her bound ok.

Hypnotizing silly women with diverse lusts: That soul tie has a grip on her that won't quit, alas.

Timothy writes to not "stir it up"--the sex instinct--until the time is right and you're ready: married.

This means you have a covenant man who's a husband. Stir it up with a loser and he tears you down.

THE POWER OF SEX AND OLDER WOMEN

FRENEMY ENABLER

Ph.D. women managed by dropout men due to a sexual soul tie, then the sexy bum moves in, aye.

Don't ever underestimate the **POWER** of sex and for an older woman the birds and bees are it.

Older monied women taken in by gigolos who take over their lives all due to a hot/sizzling soul tie.

OLDER WOMEN AND GIGOLOS

The older women lunching went crazy when "Vince" entered the room, he'd been with all of em.

Older women buy them clothes, cars, dinners; give big tips and expensive vacations for more sex.

It's the land of soul ties and the effects of broken soul ties with youtube mentors on how to survive.

Sex, sex, sex and thinking nothing of it. It's a big deal though as karma accrues with effects of it.

They all loved Vincent but he shafted me on computer work as sin effects go across the board see.

Dude can't read, don't have no job but he knows how to work that bed to keep her spiritually dead.

He's got you so twisted you've even turned down husband material you're so hep on sex devil.

You're sexually entangled. You've turned down two or three good guys as boring/no bells or whistles.

He who joins to a prostitute is one body with her for the two shall be one flesh [demonic marriage].

Soul ties are very serious. It's a hot stove taking you down an evil rabbit hole and what a toll.

FRENEMY ENABLER

Demonic soul ties affect your looks first but effects on the soul, emotions and mind are the worst.

Being so unwise you gave your youth and body to a clown who never had covenant on his mind.

Financial ties: he treats you any old way cuz he knows you need money and sex is how you pay.

Depending on an undependable person for your life provision is like living on quicksand.

HAPPY FAMILY MYTHOLOGY

I saw how they killed my rep, betrayed me with spouse, how I barely escaped, why I lost the house.

And we're supposed to love sister, our worse enemy? Jesus brought a sword to DIVIDE the family.

It's finally coming all outa me, after decades of dung holding it in you see, waiting for destiny.

People are jealous and hateful, family sins. But like mom always said it all evens out in the end.

In one week she turned mom against me, hit on my husband and ruined my reputation: calumny.

I always knew I'd have my day in court/time to speak but for then I had to hold it in, freaked.

Not until she's elderly would she see the magnitude and devastation of her sister's narcissism.

THEY HAVE NO ANCHOR

Without anchor they go along with whoever has the upper hand: that's a dumb female man.

FRENEMY ENABLER

Only pouring my emotions out on paper helped. Terse verse, timed rhymes for a little girl's yell.

They absolutely screw men in divorce courts and little sisters they've scapegoated: you go girls.

Parents screw children/children screw parents and siblings are the worst cuz they're immature first.

The movie "Baby Jane" describes it all, the merciless and ruthless antics of sisters as they fall.

And men you should be alerted, not amused, when you see this Jezebel strife in mates or muse.

SIBLING HATRED

All that hate in their low IQ souls--false accusers so bold--comes to roost as they implode.

Sibling hate, jealousy and envy are sins so they don't get off easily after harboring these things.

My hope for you is you recognize it for what it is--accept hate and go on, give up your utopian ideas.

It is possible that before you realize they hate you, you hated yourself. Your differences created guilt.

They hate because they hate, haters gonna hate, that's the only way to look at this, now relocate.

God is love but He hates those abusing His kids. God'll get em, there are consequences to sins.

A narcissistic sister is just as malicious, vindictive, manipulative and sneaky as a narc mother.

Narcissistic sisters are so highly toxic you must go no contact or before you know it life's wrecked.

FRENEMY ENABLER

She doesn't have your best interest, she's not your friend--just keep her away from your boyfriend.

SISTERS START RUMORS

Your narcissistic sister will spread rumors about you and try her best to ruin your relationship too.

She will go behind your back and sabotage with rumors your relationship and usually accomplish this.

She will plot behind the scenes how to take your man from you, or at least move you out too.

She always has a hidden agenda. She friends you only to get your information then will screw ya.

The beloved parent falls for the accusations of the narcissistic sibling: total treachery.

HEAR THEIR TAUNTING VOICE THRU LIFE

You may hear your sibling's taunting voice way into adulthood: how you're still a child, a hood.

Because of one narcissistic sibling you're cut outa the will or family business is sold in a fire sale.

She'd rather wipe out your life savings or give it to a stranger, anything to cut you out forever.

All thru childhood, adolescence, adulthood she heard the narc sister berating her in her head.

In this way, the impact of the narcissistic sibling is just as devastating as the parent believe me.

The "family needs to stick together" thing is about everyone remaining in denial, dumbing.

FRENEMY ENABLER

Not enough is said of narcissistic siblings tho' the problem's devastating with these cruel kiddies.

When the parents die we see [aghast] the pettiness of siblings as they collude with will attorney.

When I saw her unherhandedness it was difficult to let go of my first friend and sister, but I finally did.

The female narc is nosey, always taking notes. She will use it all against you later/sink your boat.

TRUST FUND TRAGEDIES

We've heard of parental abuse thru trust funds, it's ten times worse when a sibling gets control hon'

She's agreeable with what you say but then turns on a dime when away, you're in a grinder ok.

Agreeable one minute, next time you see her she's cold and silent. Good lord we're in for it now friend.

Next time you see her she's silent cuz she got what she wanted: the info to sack you and be hated.

She acted so understanding just so she could hear what's going on. I gave her the story--wrong!

When she said "I'm gonna get her!" I became scared, knowing the tenacity of women/the avengers.

It was always two against one, that's the Cinderella Syndrome--a screw job until she's finally alone.

I had to endure it to write about it: How women are the worst/two against one is the biggest curse.

NOSEY AND GOSSIPPY

FRENEMY ENABLER

Female narcs are Nosey and Gossipy. They pry in order to talk of your personal business see.

The Cinderella Syndrome is a screw job until the Prince comes to take her out and away to God.

She won't speak, she gives you the cold shoulder but she tells all about those she's jealous of.

She was nice and decent but judging you the whole time. She's killed your rep already, aye.

Ladies, be careful who you're open with. You'll see em nose into conversations like narcissists.

My sisters were so underhanded and sneaky I couldn't believe it, may they rest in peace.

The devices of liberal witches makes you frustrated and angry so anger was my defect of character.

Victimized by two liberal sisters gave me a glimpse of what men are going through in divorces.

NO RESTRAINT IN POWER PAYBACKS

Liberal sisters: without a moral guide they make up things as they go along/all about power, aye.

Not knowing how to temper power, women get mean when demonstrating it = you go girl.

Meek little ladies or meanstreaked idiots going along with the other twits? Social hypnotists.

Just as teens are cruel exacting justice, women are crueler as from centuries it all erupts.

I never knew how to talk about this since everyone knows we're supposed to love our sisters.

FRENEMY ENABLER

Jane was square-jawed, resembling mean female nazi prison guards who were hung after the war.

Narcissistic sociopathy exists in women equal to men now we're three generations into feminism.

They hate her for hating her sisters. She learns to stay calm and keep all information inside of her.

Greek Tragedies are FAMILY tragedies--all about sisters, aunts, uncles, mommies. It's all we know see.

A female narc intruding on a conversation is rude but they feel entitled to it all, they are snoops.

I WAS MUTED BY IT BUT NOW IT'S COME OUT

I was mute like a lamb to the slaughter which they mistook for weakness, ripe for soul murder.

I couldn't say anything cuz no one would believe me anyway and besides they'd only hate me.

But now it's done: my Ph.D. training, perfected method of delivery and my experiences with you honey.

For people are cruel and even worse on your way down as they join the crowd to kill a hero fallen.

Female narcs are messy: they sabotage your relationships so you can't confide in em see.

You can't tell her who you're dating cuz she'll find him and sabotage that too, there's no winning.

It's their extreme competitiveness that marks em and makes em dangerous as hell my friends.

Your boundaries are there to be busted by the narcissist so you gotta learn to enforce them firmly.

FRENEMY ENABLER

Boundaries are what save you from narcissist so just stick with it and problems will stop.

IT'S THE _REPEATED_ TRAUMA

It's the REPEATED trauma that creates the Complex PTSD characterized by painful intrusive memories.

Just when I'm happy with me, up pops the most embarrassing, humiliating memory. Agree?

The repeated trauma was him putting me down in front of everyone with them all in agreement with him.

The repeated trauma was being seen as a grasshopper in relevance when I knew I was more.

The repeated trauma was him being so arrogant as he got the whole town against me, and they agreed.

TRAUMA OF CALUMNY: GETTING EM AGAINST ME

The repeated trauma was him getting the whole family against me and I couldn't say a thing.

The repeated trauma was him--porous borders Jimmy--letting em in to rain on my parade/make a mess.

This guy was NOT my fence and he was definitely my enemy and here I thought we were married.

Prolific Writer: works all day at night, ever-ready for the inspiration to come thru and make it right.

I can hear people yelling at me and they're all women. Angry voices, ugly faces, screechin'/hollerin'.

The repeated trauma was your obvious disrespect in the face of my Scottish pride and I couldn't cope.

FRENEMY ENABLER

The repeated trauma was your misjudgments not knowing a dam thing about me, how could you.

You re-experience the memory to reject it. It's like an onion unpeeling--right now I'm at year five.

I was very happy at five years old. This was before it all hit the fan as described throughout in bold.

WHEN DID I LOSE MY UNIQUENESS

When something you care about is hindered you now have incentive to leave family/church/group.

One church recognized I had a life's work and another hindered, forbade, obstructed and mocked it.

I can write all day, think/muse looking out the window but there was a time I didn't have this freedom.

People will not let a woman work. She's expected to work for them, attend to them, worry about them.

I am very attentive to anyone human/pet in my charge but I need most time alone in my room upstairs.

Our bodies are broken down from living in households where it's fight/flight triggers every single day.

Save your money/be your own best friend to not have to depend on anyone/be jerked around like that.

PEOPLE WILL ALWAYS DISAPPOINT

Victims of dysfunction are trained to seek external validation but people ALWAYS disappoint you man.

Being my own best friend was a simple change and worked like magic. I took Karen on as a project.

FRENEMY ENABLER

Dysfunctional family: They feed/clothe you but mock and talk against you/behind your back constantly.

People will always disappoint so you must be your own best friend--take an interest in a rare gem.

I've washed you outa my mind, all you frenemies who never really knew me anyway, goodbye.

Instead of searching the net for a friend or looking up exes, just BE your friend and take an interest.

People don't get together like they did before computers--when they were expected to or forget him/her.

INSANE SOCIAL EXPECTATIONS

Those social expectations to get together ravaged my life. My mother's too--she'd drink to deal with lies.

False religion sees get-togethers and potlucks as the road to salvation the way they insist on them.

I don't like get-togethers. They bore me/piss me off with all the jealous shit shots hurting for years.

Ok witch Jezebel let me hear all about how I'm getting older now then give me advice you fat cow.

The lady said "I don't know why I was so insane around my family"--cuz we're biocomputers, literally.

Before becoming self-aware we're a robot of desires and reactions but now this is all nil/unimportant.

I have no idea why I acted that way. Cue, trigger, response, memory, defense--who knows honey.

When you're being pin-pricked and shit-shot all day it's a little hard to feel the freedom to write, ok.

FRENEMY ENABLER

Just know: the problem is they have no empathy. That's why you're in a cold land/a stranger they hate.

Overnight NEWSMAX has replaced FOX and we're happy to be rid of that fake, that's the crux.

When you're so perfect they fail to find a flaw they'll always pull the age card, that's the mob.

As old memories arise outa the fog we see what WE did not just them--that's the real growth friend.

Extreme trauma may bring depersonalization--you split from SELF/become a different ugly person.

LOST SPIRIT ADAPTING TO DISRESPECT

I lost my true spirit for decades adapting to their disrespect and I spiraled down, a wreck.

God restored my spirit and said He loved my peculiarities. God wants us unique not EVER conforming.

I'm here for your entertainment and edification while you're at it and I really hope you enjoy it.

Somehow she thought she was equalizing with men by being promiscuous and that explains it.

Having been told men and women are alike and there are no lines she became an [unconscious] slut.

Isn't it wonderful--after all that sinning all we have is our perfect works for history, fortunately.

My future is perfectly mapped out for me as long as I stay sin-free, it's a divine groove with the King.

When I found out it was all about sex I was shocked. You mean to tell me that's all they think about?

FRENEMY ENABLER

Because of addiction she was hooked to old systems who wouldn't let her up and it was tragic she said.

We're ALL sinners--Jesus said no one's good, only God. Multiply that times your age = we're ALL flawed.

The jealous say you're ungrateful so you become over-grateful then they say you're a crazy weasel.

They made me so sick to my stomach I had school phobia and now it's just a hatred of anything social.

The traumatized split self was so depersonalized I took on another name and other culture, terrified.

SHIFTING SANDS OF DYSFUNCTION

The shifting sands in dysfunctional families can be more terrifying than a natural disaster, I mean it.

Betrayals from jealousy triangles, sterile dynasties and narcissistic competitions break down our body.

After being serially attacked by extreme jealous hatred for years, my skin just hung on me/I was in tears.

Is there anything more lethal than female jealousy? The lengths she goes to get back are deadly.

The I Ching says "return tot he right path, no blame". Well it's the same thing for us cuz Jesus came.

One reasons memories hurt is because we're mature now so looking back really smarts far more.

Cuz they didn't know who you were they made a big deal outa nothing but then, sadly, you took it on.

SHAME marks the disease decades after recovery. She can't get over it, it suffocates her constantly.

FRENEMY ENABLER

She had Buddha statues everywhere though she's not a Buddhist but wants the image of a goodist.

The hate you with a hatred they can't describe nor understand. It possesses them man.

But menacing, harassing memories can be erased by refocusing on Jesus. I had success with this.

Jesus was with you on it all, He knows how you were tempted/what happened so talk to Him.

I don't necessarily want a sickeningly sweet smoothie with ten dates in it but my cells do so I drink it.

COMPLEX PTSD BRINGS MEMORY INTRUSION

The characteristic of repeated humiliation is memory-intrusion and they can be hellish/no fun.

Don't be dumb girl he's made it very clear what he wants without which you're a witch he will ditch.

From rampant greed and selfishness people screw each other over in a narcissistic society like this.

The narcissist uses humiliation to put you down so he can be up. That means PUBLIC ignominy, gossip.

Must face the mean things we did once getting the upper hand--unconscious devices in past systems.

Once knowing who they are never give em a chance to impose on you cuz you're screwed if they do.

The relationship to a narcissist is horrible because of the public ignominy and humiliation central to it.

Tho' it appeared I did nothing for 26 years, all alone my mind expanded light years ahead of others.

FRENEMY ENABLER

Strangely interesting quips act as little releasors of old anchors from the past or the gutter.

Just **ONE** good selfie, not a million. Get some class, come on--it's just narcissism all around.

Lady said "my loving Mormon husband became an ugly treacherous alcoholic with the devil in him".

When it came to your addiction, which came first--your mother's hatred/gossip or the crutch hon'?

Narcissists use humiliation of victims, by definition. The more people hear about it the better son.

NO one believed me about him, how he was torturing me in private while portraying me as the savage.

SO WEAKENED I SUCCUMBED

I was so weakened by him and his calumnies all I could do is succumb to this frame-up he invented.

He died decades back but his influence remains in a positive way writing about these family facts.

He made me so miserable living under the same roof I felt I was in hell but to outsiders, there's no proof.

I just wanna stay in my castle/never leave til the day I die. I've made it this far but can't take it anymore.

I nicknamed him Jolly Jimmy cuz that's how he was to outsiders but in the home he was a disaster.

He drank wine from the time he got up and his son drank beer. On TV was constant ballgames/cheers.

I became a non-entity that didn't exist. My audacity, charm and looks faded along with all this.

FRENEMY ENABLER

He would cleverly insult me at my weakest points about looks or how I had no friends, totally forsook.

Being mad at the deceased is just as body-destroying so we just gotta forgive it all then go on.

Once I lost audacity I lost him since that was the attraction. I couldn't defend SELF against him.

I can still recall stomach aches of pure dismay over another sad, terrifying day with my mate.

HORRORS: LIVING WITH SATANIC ADDICTION

Horrors: living in relation to a satanic addiction like alcoholism! Alcohol is a conduit to "him".

Lady said "my two husbands were impotent--one from alcoholism, the other from prostate cancer".

Generally a whoremonger becomes very ugly and craggy in his sixties, that's divine karma baby.

Don't abuse your husband by using him as a therapist. Women tend to do this--cater to him more sis.

In an abusive marriage the doctor said my organs were working at 10%--I was depleted, spent.

EVIL SISTERS AND CINDERELLA

When the evil sisters saw he hated their sister they gave him large sums of money, that was his training.

He became hyper-loyal to the two sisters and her future was mapped out in an emotional gutter.

From that point on all decisions were made behind closed doors with him part of the elites drinking beer.

FRENEMY ENABLER

It's what you call an inveterate system, obdurate as hell. Unchanging, she's a helpless victim in her shell.

I know what it's like to have your life sucked right out this way, thru a destroyed reputation: calumny.

Life is hell in a system like this but due to weakness all thoughts of escape/happiness are dismissed.

There's little difference between a mean prison guard tormenting you and your own husband Sue.

Apparently God put me thru these circumstances to write about it and I've done that as promised.

My Emotional Intelligence [EI] was gone--having laid down my life to him I was hardly renowned.

HAVING AGREED TO GRASSHOPPER STATUS

Having agreed to my grasshopper status and censoring, the light was gone and that's really ugly.

Right after I survived him I attracted a gang of boys who imposed on me. Lord: social muscle needed.

Having been sheltered God put me through these events to make me hep and tough, boundaries up.

For a female writer all energy should go into either writing or housework. Home is all or be cursed.

After going thru that abuse I see the importance of a Happy Homelife cuz from hell comes strife.

It appeared the most important thing to my sisters was to destroy me forever and erase me: censured.

But since they did the same thing to their husbands and mom I no longer take it personally/I've grown.

FRENEMY ENABLER

It was so horrible living with Jolly Jimmy I can feel it in my gut as I describe the sickening treachery.

Suddenly my step-sons hated me--his kids. This became cruel cuz you know how they are the twits.

Sisters and Jolly Jimmy as sick systems connect together. Left one to start another, self asunder.

These women were in control yet knew nothing. Their only knowledge was in slogans, commie.

EVIL STEPMOTHER SYNDROME

The step-kids were more than I. could stand--I never asked for this hatred, disdain, despising.

My step-son had said "I despise you" in my living room. Out of the blue. I don't need this from you.

I don't know that I could take the Stepmother Syndrome again and it's even worse with girls in sin.

They fell into God's disfavor later. Both died at an early age/gone forever while now you're the sage.

They found they could weasel in/cause trouble thru my sisters: here we nave interlocking jealousies.

All these interconnecting systems in my early life taught me lessons I'll never forget/they're encrypted.

We live in two houses cuz we're both thinkers and have different hours and see solitude as superior.

Apparently God put me thru these circumstances to write about it and I've done that as promised.

Someone's gonna come in, team a masterpiece, fix the ship and be the financial wizard quick.

FRENEMY ENABLER

P.S. A genius is compelled to rhyme since the words are connected thru both meaning *AND* sound.

I messed up when reflecting my generation. I grew up when transcending them and all their friends.

Things have changed and liberals are shocked, dismayed and irrelevant. Some may seek you to explain it.

What liberalism has always done is seek the wisdom of pagans. Imagine that: sinking to such low stations.

Paganism seeks to eliminate guilt but that's necessary for the fall into humility and then being rebuilt.

The illness is characterized by denial so how'd I know I was wrong but years later I felt remorse over the trials.

The new age goes mainline when you hear them say "I'm spiritual but I'm not religious": that's the occultists.

SEX USED AS A BATTERING RAM AGAINST WEST

The issue of sexuality is used as a battering ram against Western culture to destroy it altogether.

You either worship the creation (in infinite ways) or the Creator who is blessed forever: simplify with the latter.

God through Trump will expose the backroom deals of the court, a great light to the whole world once more.

They love the earth: "interplanetary coming together". Behind it is occult spirituality: demons/stormy weather.

Paganism is no longer called "new age" but rather "progressive spirituality" and it's globalism: not ok.

Modernity itself is a worldview on the nature of existence which is thoroughly pagan.

FRENEMY ENABLER

The entire worldview since the hippies ("we are one" B.S.) is based on paganism. The solution: TWO-ISM.

Power of rationalization drives the culture war. They must lambast/overstate to enforce views/make sure.

A yes person is a miserable watered down wasteland. He's lost his Self so needs boring events planned.

Puppy knows mommy has two sides so he doesn't act to bring that out-- that's how God works, no doubt.

WE'RE ALL GOD: HOW SILLY THIS SAYING

One-ism destroys God's blessings and light totally. It's *Him* not we're "one" like we're all God--how silly.

Hindu means "not two"--formed in opposition to a separate God discerning good/evil and loving me and you.

One-ism says you're God--but you don't look/smell like Him: the most absurd generation ever been.

Hindu is committed to breaking the distinction between God and man, making it all one: How boring and bland.

Hindu wants to bring God down to man at his will. But God blesses who He wants, He sees who steals/kills.

Paganism—one-ism--is joining opposites in bath/locker rooms and here we see the insanity in full bloom.

If God is in us all-one, who's gonna bless us? God is separate so He blessed me with things precious.

If you wanna save society preach two-ism: It's not about being "nice" but pleasing God/repenting of vice.

Because I love Him as separate, holy and superior, beckoning/leaning on Him, He extravagantly blessed me.

FRENEMY ENABLER

Two-ism not one-ism: I wanna worship God as separate so He can bless and shed His light on me!

One-ism/paganism has taken over our culture for 50 years. See the signs and return to God in good cheer.

If you wanna make it in life, work and please God. For He has plans to prosper and not to hurt you though you're "odd".

A pagan worldview is based on fantasies which get increasingly weirder but to which we're forced to adhere.

Hindu means "not two" but two there are and thank you God it's true: you're separate from an evil herd.

DENIAL OF BINARIES IS PURE B.S.

Look out for pagan terms: "denial of binaries, discovering non-dual reality, joining dichotomies/opposites."

Preach two-ism and God will reward you greatly for bringing the focus back on Himself, the All Mighty.

Worship creation (in infinite ways) or love the Creator one way, all day: That's the way to high pay.

Unlike the kids, a genius can never view things through the social prism. End up alone, whatever, amen.

I can condense all this cuz I know the difference between God and me, or me thinking I'm God with out Thee.

The fall: A childhood lost, an adulthood gained and a journey into maturity while being caned.

Ask em "why wouldn't you want someone to be good?" and they're theory falls apart--can't defend, no heart.

Holy means separate. Set apart, playing an important part, sanctified by God with gifts infinite.

FRENEMY ENABLER

Pagan Gods are a mere extension of humanity and they are homosexual uniting opposites he and she.

God is all about charming differences not boring and militant homogenization or skittish similitude.

Why do crazy liberals love systems of slavery and push them so haughtily? They know nothing of reality.

Proven but when you mention it they'll come against you for saying it: they aren't mature enough to take it.

SICKEST AND MOST PERVERTED GENERATION

This will go down as the sickest/most perverted generation even beyond Hitler's at least they had genders.

Liberals are perverts. Don't tell me this is always how it's been. We were a decent country back then.

Liberals are about including but I'm about dividing: attacking heresies, mythologies and false ideologies.

501c3 opens the door to the counterfeit spirit--that's when in church you don't like it, even fear it.

Five percent of churches are not under the money system so they are the remnant soon to be eminent.

Anyone who says Christians shouldn't vote (partake in our system) is helping Satan: we must resist him.

I'm a Christian who never went to church--could it be because it was part of what I sensed had emerged?

If church is like the society I'm escaping by going to church, what a letdown as God will never come first.

What comes first in the false church? Being social, "loving" people but not God's power/shunning evil?

FRENEMY ENABLER

For victory there are things to do on our end: Intercede, pray, assert, expose, make Christian friends.

A 501C3 church is unequally yoked to government, Islam, wicca, Satan, Planned Parenthood/pro-choice.

PEOPLE MOURN WHEN THE WICKED RULE

People really mourn when the wicked rule. For a lesson in Civics these last 8 years were the best school.

The false church marked by liberal drift is now taking down crosses/letting muslims in as if they fit.

I'll never stop talking/thinking about the Obama years: the daily trauma and disappointment, and the fears.

Obama years taught us about government, tyranny, globalism, liberalism and the new age generation.

Who knew the value of freedom until it was lost? Who knew what tyranny was before a tyrant was boss?

The Obama years weren't only scary but also dirty. Dark perversions, unheard of things, revulsions.

That whole entitled generation of leftists politicians were hawkish, nasty, dirty, whorish, brutish, outlandish.

Conservatives couldn't get tenure, we were looked down on by globalist pawns, arrogant though dumb.

There were no conservatives lecturing on campus and if so you had to have several armed guards. Hard.

For 8 years the smart had to endure insults from young upstarts calling us "stupid, bigot"--with no heart.

The leftist politicians (friends of Barry O) dressed fashionably chic--did that make them seem smart, ya think?

FRENEMY ENABLER

It started in the sixties, a 50 year war: changes hard to endure but it amped up and now popped, for sure.

We never knew how dirty leftism got until it culminated in Obama's reign of terror/commie fervor.

Even in the 70's we were attacked in colleges for being Christian or conservative, seen as silly and foolish.

I've been attacked by feminists for my words. They yelled and even hit me if no one was around to observe.

HIPPYISM HIT GLITCHES AND BECAME WITCHES

Hippyism came to it's ugly head and hit glitches but now they're digging in to enforce will of witches.

You talk about ugly and dark--what the kids have done for decades and we enabled it "it's all ok".

The declension into chaos and dissension was so gradual we just got dense but now--wow! awakened at last!

False church always declines through one-ism. All of them--when the two-ists leave/never come again.

They were so stiff-necked and haughty, so mean if you didn't agree, so social while you were a rare anomaly.

Liberals don't seem to be changing or waking up but rather digging in--perhaps that's the way with sin?

Liberals use obscenities--"F" talk to increase their base with losers I guess. Why else speak in a filthy mess?

It is so shocking to hear an "expert" use the F word--but it's common and they insist it's no problem.

Sometimes F talk gets a laugh, sometimes it doesn't go over at all and the result is rejection/it's rough.

FRENEMY ENABLER

It's definitely crossing a line, then compelled to increase it to justify it and that's how all sin works, believe it.

The corruption of boys is the greatest delight in the homosexual pagan heart all through history (creates misery).

If they took 'f**kin' out they wouldn't be saying anything: those dumb nuts from the crazy left wing.

Liberals wish to banish us as a country. They're globalists and that means no-borders and tyranny.

GLOAL BARRACKS OR A RIGHT TO BE DIFFERENT?

It's time to stop turning us into global barracks--we've a right to be different. Vladimir Putin, love 'im.

And to think I was brought up/baptized in the Methodist church, haven for heretics, homosexual, /illegal aliens.

Darkness ain't about skin color. It's dirty, horrible, ungodly, devilish squalor yet a "constitutional scholar".

It's hard to believe it's the churches causing all the trouble, taking in a cult that hates us/of the devil.

We in the right brain are seen as unreliable. What we see as productive puttering they see as unviable.

For those who are called "irresponsible" let me ask you one thing: Do you take care of your animals?

While he was playing golf and spending our mint on vacations we were suffering all his regulations.

Our hopes and aspirations will never again go on deaf ears as they were by a queer, think of that dear.

We're gonna have so much money, we're gonna celebrate and party cuz we're free for eternity, so happy.

FRENEMY ENABLER

A populist reversed 60 years of globalism--amazing.

We worried for 8 years, of course we're tired. Anyone is when dominated by thieves, traitors and liars.

The main media hates American people, works for global elites and is covering up a satanic pedophile ring.

I guess it's best to just party for 40 days and nights until The Man gets in to clean up the terrible blight.

Get this to avoid having the blues: The main news is the fake news, the fake news is the main news.

Are you with the herd of socially hypnotized mal-adaptants, liberals, neo-cons or false churchist get-alongs?

ENTRY POINTS FOR DEMONS: WARNING

Watch entry points to the devil and his demons. What you do, watch, experience and let in are some reasons.

Trump said he would expose all of em not just the queen of the Satanic Worldwide Pedophile Ring.

Being delusional doesn't make you a winner, it means you've been conned. That's no great identity, c'mon!

Look up, look UP then LOOK UP.

Keep looking UP all day and night thanking God He removed the blight.

Quitting your church: Where is that line--when they remove crosses/change to mosques--what is the sign?

The Catholic church was infiltrated by pedophile rings and that's how they're controlled: they're framed, cold.

Muslim TV gives tips on how to apply makeup over abuse scars. Liberals say "it's ok--it's just their culture".

FRENEMY ENABLER

Trump is talking $1 gas and already this has come to pass!

Why does Obama shower love on our enemies? Castro is liberal chic. Ted Cruz

Why does the left make excuses for monsters like Castro? To maintain identity, he'd become a symbol.

There's an impulse on the left to defend totalitarianism and it makes me so nervous about them.

The most important word is no. It clears the way for the highest in your day so don't say Yes, no pains to allay.

ISIS calls for random knife attacks but still the libtards want open borders even the kids and college hacks.

Then the players would cry during our anthem cuz they knew how blessed they were to be here, amen?

THE TRUTH IS STRANGER THAN FICTION

The truth is stranger than fiction: It's surrealistic as events unfold in this, the second American Revolution.

The loudest isn't the majority so don't worry. Just a little while longer and we'll have victory/they'll be sorry.

Mean leaders start big wars when they're about to be overthrown and Hillary's the worst ever known.

It makes me sick to hear them actually equate Donald with that pervert. He's a prince but they want her.

Sex crimes with children/child exploitation: That's the worst but not to the herd which accepts abortion.

Our culture's already made dense through abortion-acceptance and thus there isn't more shock/uproar.

Accepting the unacceptable has made us dense: Once the conscience is gone we're a moral dunce.

FRENEMY ENABLER

Liberalism, based on a false premise, became more inveterate and extreme so now we're a sewer and mean.

For anyone who doubts Trump (due to hype) just listen to his speeches. If still in doubt I'm speechless.

PURITANISM A REACTION TO DEBAUCHERY

Puritanism: a reaction to 18th c. debauchery and that accounts for American decency, until recently.

How does this corruption happen? 1 an uneducated public 2 no term limits 3 a bought off/criminal media.

Going against the grain is the way to be free. Constructive anger immediately brings creativity.

He's a military vet with cancer. Give him a break when you ask a question and get an angry answer.

Smart man: The Art of the Deal. First, you salvage. Second, you're savage.

They love Hillary and wanna kill babies. I say take back the vote from these creepy so-called ladies.

Art of the Deal: Fire a person a day if not quite good enough. That's why he's the best/takes no guff.

Wonderful president lovin' on Houston--this is salve on our wounds not salt like fake news is tellin'

Our own media rooting for North Korea against our president? Incredible but that's how they do it.

They may be brainwashed/out of control but still a reality: they mean business and are hard/cold.

Lower IQ means lower impulse control, more in the moment--tastes good while nutrition is absent.

FRENEMY ENABLER

Come unglued when strategies don't work but because they've been brainwashed, can't relearn.

She dresses provocatively so that the male stops thinking, is sexually aroused and then captured.

Sex, then a noose around his neck for 18 years: child support (or jail if he fails) so men: stay aware.

Hypersexuality is the downfall of Western civilization.

POSTMODERNISM IS FAMILY FRANKENSTEIN

The usual postmodern mosaic is a stitched-together family frankenstein and it's destroying society.

History shows niceness gets you killed.

In fatherless homes the girl may hypersexualize and the boys aggressive.

Japanese families stay together and you don't see girl hypersexuality or boy aggressiveness.

You can see it in how females love bad boys. Aggression even turns em on rather than terrifies/annoys.

Bad boys get lotsa sex in the era of crumbling families. Everyone knows about girls with no daddies.

When you see a pretty girl you know some guy is putting up with her now.

Hypersexuality is a reproductive strategy to shatter the family, furthered by welfare and feminism.

If you don't do their thing and go to their gatherings they don't wanna see ya: the group's everything.

The fatherless girl doesn't know why she's hyper-sexualized, nor the boy why he's become aggressive.

FRENEMY ENABLER

In war the aggressive male will protect and the hypersexualized girl reproduce: why they choose.

Crumbling families means war to the biobrain then symptoms roll out of her hypersex and his aggression.

Feminism has created hypersexual females/aggressive males by wrecking family in our recent history.

Never trust a liberal over 3, especially a republican. Ann Coulter

THE GREAT DETERMINER DECIDES FATE OF NATIONS

There is a great Determiner who decides the fate of nations.

Immaturity is a sort of cognitive impairment: Thinking isn't fully developed, yet they control government?

Altercations are all over politics--there's something about liberty-lovers that erks those thick as bricks.

You know you're superior if their thoughts are just like the club's. Forget these plebs they'll only snub.

Because of what you went through you're now a certain way. From aura to voice they can't take you, ok?

If they don't put you first, hell with em' cuz it hurts the heart and makes everything so much worse.

Science is not determined by majority vote nor consensus, but continual re-evaluation of the facts.

The corrupt military tactic of tyrannies, a disgrace: to deny they're doing it while they do it in your face.

Old guard liberals like Pelosi are still arrogant (doing crazy things) but that'll surely come back to bite em.

Need convalescence after the traumas of life: having to take that from dummies whether husband/wife.

FRENEMY ENABLER

Conservatives put down for decades. They're seen through negative lens while "loving liberals" get accolades.

A.A. is a liberal social club. I don't see how people stay sober in there/many conservatives feels snubbed.

LIBERALISM IS A MENTAL/SPIRITUAL DISORDER

Liberalism is a mental/spiritual disorder. In the name of tolerance they're the most intolerant, for starters.

Replaced Christian absolutism for cultural relativism and for decades have gone in the opposite direction.

A "liberal Christian"is a dangerous, phony and pathetic oxymoron.

There's been a falling away, a drought. The church is a traitor, glad to be out.

Your church is great maybe but there's a falling away generally.

Please grant us patience and fortitude as we plod through these next few days while we wait for our glory raised.

Knowing they're ill allows you to respond (know what's coming) not react (cuz they're so disappointing).

Spiritually ill makes them mentally ill. Sin brings insanity. Repent, symptoms dissolve/you can make a dent.

If you don't know Christian absolutism is right, you'll slide into relativism which is devastation overnight.

Because they're ill they're in denial. They're in denial because they're ill.

Liberals in shock: "Oh no, we're not gonna have any abortions". What a weird, sick and strange reaction.

They always wanna take a pot shot in social gatherings. I'm gonna avoid these stressful dissemblings.

FRENEMY ENABLER

They get you in front of other people and embarrass you. That's the social world, more than I can chew.

Liberals always corrected our speech. They were the superiors, always ready to teach about the breach.

Before Trump we didn't have a comeback. We just accepted what they said and then there was Barrack.

APPEASEMENT EMBOLDENS AGGRESSORS

Appeasement always emboldens an aggressor. An aggressor sniffs out weakness and dictators all know her.

Don't argue with them. You now know all about em: adults acting like children and kids echoing.

Their God is their leftist ideology. Without that all hope is gone and about what they did: no apologies.

There's ignorance and apathy, then political correctness creates the perfect storm camouflaged by sympathy.

A constitutional republic is altogether wrong for an immoral people.

Democracy always ends in dictatorship or anarchy. The Founding Fathers never intended that, surely.

Hollywood is licking it's ego wounds like the media. They can't believe you didn't listen to them like idiots.

Actors who can't keep their lives together were convinced they knew better cuz it was on TV to the letter.

They start shooting yelling "Allahu Akbar" and the officials say "we just don't know the motive yet".

It doesn't matter who the shooter is--blame the gun.

See the system: You were compelled to do it but they turned it around/you were blamed/couldn't intuit.

FRENEMY ENABLER

Never have we had more soft, disconnected ivy leaguers running us, always thinking they're better than us.

Rather than being thrilled if someone notices you why not look up to God cuz they don't have a clue!

I love the Lord like most liberty-lovers. We obey only Him and He gives us all great rewards and favor.

Obama didn't go on news with low viewers. He goes on comedy shows with race-bating narratives.

I'm not gonna battle your monitoring of my utterances/political stances cuz you're one of the dunces.

DESPERATE NEED FOR APPROVAL

You think it's "nice" to tell people lies all so they'll like you and not see your silly (fake friendly) disguise?

Anything clubby I hate. Unless it's my own club of those who wanna learn about synchronicity/high fate.

The ivy league pseudo-intellectual skinny tie wearers are gonna show you, the bitter clingers.

They're not encroaching nor have anything to do with us but to block Trump let's have a war with Russia.

Brazen, unapologetic corruption.

The left like Podesta are gonna lean on Electors just as the mafia leans on judges to be defectors.

This is all about dems not wanting to leave office and Geo Soros doubling his funding for anti-Trumping.

Waste, over-reach, bureaucratic spread.

If I went to the middle east and felt offended at religious symbolism would they change it all for me?

FRENEMY ENABLER

It's limited election: God doesn't call everyone.

Now's the time to pray, for they were even planning on stealing the election and giving it to Hillary.

Black unemployment doubled under Obama, Trump's calling for investment in mainly black urban areas.

Now they're complaining Trump came to their communities? Obama never went he just created enemies.

Promises: Trump's putting the best people in place to deliver us but liberals see it as a major crisis.

Graciousness, intelligence, class.

Women never deserve to be hit but feminist thinking can create a short fuse in men or anyone you twit.

UPSIDE DOWN WORLD OF OPPOSITES

It's an upside down world of opposites. When you hear Infowars is the worst it means they're the best.

Arguing with liberal feminists puts anyone on edge. Either they shrivel up in fear or fight with the bitch.

Guilty: Liberal victims and their assault on America. Ann Coulter

Arrogant female politicians betraying in a man's game. Men don't do that, knowing they'll get the same.

If they're naive/watch fake news they'll see you as weird cuz there's a lot different about info-nerds.

Give me liberty or give me death. Patrick Henry

Reverse captivity, restore fortunes

All you can do is start your own fan club. To hell with them/their bad influence: work filled with flubs.

FRENEMY ENABLER

He's gonna bomb the hell outa ISIS right after his inauguration! As a surprise after our 8 year destruction.

Obama's track record: weak, indecisive, and never taking action.

Trump said "some" not "all" but people are so dumbed down they see him as racist and I'm appalled.

History will not be kind to Barrack Obama

Forget your crazy siblings, your mother and father loved you: apple of their eye/thought you were cute.

National Academy of Television Arts and Sciences is Satan spelled backwards--to hell with the "stars".

If they're at war against us but we're not at war against them, they're winning. Rudy Guilliani

Right and reps: freedom, liberty, property/gun rights. Left and dems: big government control: too high a price.

Los Angeles/New York Times want to abolish electoral college to neutralize white rural folk. Disgusting, no joke.

DEMS: POWER IN THE CITIES/WIPE OUT FARMING COMMUNITIES

Democrats want power in the cities filled with minorities while voting out white farmers in the country.

White privilege = bad. Diversity = good. They peddle that all day cuz they need minorities for livelihood.

16 million in NYC and half are minorities. Add to that Chicago, L.A.--of course dems want straight vote, ok?

When dealing with barbarians just gotta kill em.

Never cave into white-shaming! White-hatred, cop-hatred and America-hatred is just democrat training.

FRENEMY ENABLER

While we go into our new glory days the left is regressing into more insane behavior, as always.

The belligerent left wants to plunge us into war before he gets in. Trump wants peace, to just talk to Putin.

THE LEFT ARE MEGALOMANIACS

The left are megalomaniacs who can't accept they've been removed. Trump's aware of this, amused.

Trump's accomplished more before even getting into office than Obama did in eight years (just lawless).

Politics's downstream from culture. Expect a cultural shift as Hollywood's in the pits: make right wing hits!

It's an artificial divide created by Hollywood. Forget their politics, just see reality--do you think you could?

Glenn Beck has gone to the left, he hates Trump and he's daft.

Christians didn't live their religion, but you see Muslims do live theirs--thus filling the inevitable vacuum.

Christians may have caved in with every family quarrel over reality--and thus this cultural tragedy.

Establishment churches are helping subvert this country and keep Christians from fighting evil--abode of devils.

You watch people who you know are crooked, racist, mentally deranged but because they're on TV it's ok.

You must be strong to be in the public eye today. Liberals are scum and will stoop to any level to degrade.

He's got his hand in your pocket and has taken away the shield for your safety. Cursed for being informed.

Stretched thin due to over-generosity.

FRENEMY ENABLER

Crimes are in the democrat run cities not us white rural folk but they wanna take our guns/put us in a yoke.

Spoiled, dangerous brats are for full tyranny to continue their meal ticket. They haven't had Civics, think about it.

They really believe the average Trump supporter's like the KKK cuz they listen to news media all day.

CONTINUOUS LYING OF FAKE NEWS ALL DAY

Female competition: feminists don't help em up but keep em down: size em up then gossip all over town.

Not about saving the earth but shutting businesses down to ship em to China cuz that's the globalist plan.

"Everythig is perfect in its own right". This is the biggest bull from the left which we must fight.

Must make aesthetic judgments again--of higher/lower, better/best, worst/less but that's "racism" I guess.

Weakness emboldens aggressors and you can't win a war without identifying the enemy (homelife messers).

Political correctness, ignorance is bliss, multiculturalism, new tolerance: At some point we gotta dump this.

Co-exist mentalities create tragedies. The left says it's about poverty and oppression not terrorism, really?

The only shocking thing left in life is the truth and it doesn't get more shocking than that. Michael DelGriorno

Obama's not crazy or stupid, he's devout.

First they populate then infiltrate all sectors even cops--then they wage war for total control, to be tops.

The left are volitionally slaves: When dependent on government they control you from birth to graves.

FRENEMY ENABLER

Multiculturalism has become a god and religion--a false one.

The New Tolerance demands you accept it but also validate it, even become it and as for your belief, deny it.

Only the saints feel remorse. The rest could care less: they are shameless--called a seared conscience.

THE MORE TYRANNICAL THE QUICKER WE WAKE UP

The more tyrannical they get the faster people are waking up.

Their draconian measures slipped through in the dead of night shows their desperation--we're in a critical transition.

It's so easy to be generous with someone else's money.

Poets rule culture, the others talk too much.

Many husbands are generous to all but their wife--a drive for social acceptance supersedes personal life.

"White privilege" is how they make your kids hate themselves for being themselves.

Every animal on the planet knows there are two sexes, except the people of San Francisco. Michael Savage

Social world is all about events. But I don't wanna go cuza how I feel, how could I know? I just stay home.

After the event they said "he looked old/bloated". Why go to the event if the gossip pegs you/its encoded.

The event's over and no one remembers it. Why go? I've never understood that. It's not about Obama's "legacy" but handing Trump a crisis.

With Trump elected millions felt a "portal to a new world" open. A release of fear and for once we felt hopeful.

FRENEMY ENABLER

Liberals used to be against wars and the police state. Now they love wars and hate.

Rioting has become fashionable in America, and it's powered by the left--we know that/it's relevant.

Soon Obama's just a footnote in history.

You can't compromise with people who want you erased from the face of the earth. Lou Pate

To describe how Obama destroyed our country it would take a library of books not just a short thesis.

GOOD LEADERS HATE UNJUST GAIN

Good leaders hate unjust gain.

Hillary and Obama moved us toward war. Trump: the peace candidate for prosperity/peace and so much more.

Reach out to liberals by saying "your party is a warmongering psycho group now".

They showed you who they were in 2016, now don't forget in 2017.

It is regrettable that the Obama Admin is ending it's term in this manner. Nevertheless I offer New Year greetings. Putin

Paul Ryan is disgraceful trash, un-American filth. Alex Jones

Obama has sabotaged us from the beginning--that's what globalism is: making us weak, never winning.

New AXIS of Trump's America, Putin's Russia and European populists to squash liberalism for good.

We've turned the tide but the battle is only just heating up. Alex Jones

Trendies won't visit parents in nursing homes but love foreigners and know what celebrities eat for dinner.

FRENEMY ENABLER

"I coulda won". Obama's so petty, diminishing the stature of the Whitehouse: not a heavy, but deadly.

Democrats side with the Muslims--wanting to give them land all over: add to that Merkel bringing in millions.

The lame duck should put everything on cruise control and let things work out--not create obstacles and pout.

OBAMANOIDS MORE DANGEROUS THAN GANGSTERS

Politicians like Obama are far more dangerous than gangsters. Michael Savage

Neo-Cons are just like liberals: they want war with Russia (who has done nothing)

All over the world Obama's being dissed. He's perpexed but gladly all his antics are dismissed.

Putin's so clever: using the sanctions as occasion to invite children to a New Year's Eve party at the Kremlin.

Obama has been so weakened he's become increasingly irrelevant, people don't care and hate the petulant.

A modern gang member and mental patient: Would this be liberals by chance, calling it "justice"?

Obama's like a kid who'd been given a perfect and brilliantly intricate watch, took it all apart and called it "success".

Russia and the U.S. are at peace with each other and have been for a long time. Liberals are stuck in 60's crimes.

Special interests want war and Obama is their man. The goal of global domination is crashing with these plans.

Evil people always want to gin up wars.

FRENEMY ENABLER

As he's leaving the party he throws a stink bomb into the crowd, setting stage for disorder/a dark cloud.

Causing as much damage as he can as he goes out the door.

Obama provoked Putin (the Judo expert) who just stepped aside and let him fall under his own pressure.

WEAK LEADERS CREATE DISASTER

There's no predicting what a desperate weak leader might do. He gets worse each day and seems hysterical too.

He's raising the boiling point to give himself a job—save the world from what he created, the slob.

Putin is the strong man who didn't take the bait. Smooth, not irate.

Any Russian hacking just exposed that evil criminal Hillary so we should thank them for the pillory.

He's a political corpse whose administration is a bunch of angry shallow-brained losers. Vladimir Putin aids.

Never has this happened before, it's a first. Most presidents sail through transition but this guy's the worst.

A man like Obama can never admit he's wrong. He's pokin' Putin to get a reaction.

There's no difference between neo-cons and liberals. So now there's a fight in the steer house of RNC politicos.

Their foot will slide in due time (Moses). 8 years God never left nor forsook us and now He has saved us.

Neo-Cons wanna steer the Trump ship right to where it'd be if won by Hillary.

Obama won the Nobel Peace Price cuza the commies in the U.N.--they're both the same: one.

FRENEMY ENABLER

The ugliness of what he's doing to the voters and to mess up the Trump reign causes fear/frustration.

FLAWED ARGUMENTS NEED BIG GOVERNMENT

Deport the 28% illegal alien prisoners first, that's simple.

Their arguments are flawed and unpersuasive so they need big gov to give them advantage/in place of.

Flawed arguments resort to crony capitalism.

It doesn't matter how big and strong something looks, that's a paper tiger. It's about morals/wisdom/fiber.

The establishment churches are worse than atheists. Alex Jones

It hasn't gotten better it's gotten worse. But clear minds see the synthesis which ends in a hearse.

It was your demonization of Trump that got him elected, losers.

You go build your hell together, we'll build our heaven together.

Putin turned the other cheek and took the high road: that's the difference between a prince and a toad.

Oh my, the devastation Obama has done to the democrat party--nation, state and local! Thank you loony loco.

If they can keep Putin calm and just shrug this off, Obama ends up with so much egg on his face/a bluff.

Obama doesn't want our good relations with a prior enemy to solve our common problems and needs to be free.

Obama knows it's in our best interest to ally with Russia given the Middle East. He pushes that away--see?

Don't worry! Trump's and Putin's mutual dislike of Obama will come together in pure street savvy (be happy).

FRENEMY ENABLER

This is not aimed toward Russia but the presidency of Donald J. Trump. Dangerous punt by just a grunt.

This has been going on for four years and now, 20 days before you leave office, you take action by destruction?

He's trying to kill the Trump Administration before it even begins.

If Trump wins will they activate rioters or blow something up and blame it on us? Got no guts, just nuts.

In the hopes they'd back down Wikileaks gave just a little but if stubborn they'd give us the horrible.

You can tell by his speeches what a wonderful man and intelligence he is. If they can't, good riddance.

LANDSLIDES CAN'T BE STOLEN BUT THEY TOOK THE REST OF EM

Landslides can't be stolen. Like a miracle of biblical proportions our guy will take it as victory rolls in.

If we win the big banks and special interests lose. If they win the people lose--it's just that simple. Donald Trump

100 years democrats have ruled inner cities. They're a bombed out war zone from plans like Hillary's.

Inner cities are dangerous, the education stinks and no jobs. Thank democrats for that, the slobs.

You can't compare Trump--a wonderful man--with a pervert and known pedophile like Hillary Clinton.

Wicked on the inside but covered with a persona allowing them to operate fully and go free besides.

Lynch the apologizer for Hillary Clinton has plead the fifth against self-recrimination: we're losing our nation.

FRENEMY ENABLER

Election was unbearable--excruciating actually. Let's keep in touch, we've been on this ride together, anxiously.

Our only hope is the NYPD and the FBI rank and file, both disgusted but are they brave enough to pursue it?

OBAMA WAS DAILY TRAUMA

The administration of Obama was daily trauma but that brought a revolution back to Americana Nirvana.

It's black vs. white: There's no lukewarm here (it's divided friends and families) for it's EPIC/see victory tonite.

Hillary: Justice delayed is not justice denied.

Feminine virtue and character vs. modern women: coarseness, vulgarity, superficiality and selfishness.

Today's the day: for the Trump victory and the gallos for Hillary. She's the devil we overcame, truthfully.

Creepy liberals: When I make a comment I turn off notifications--hell if I'm gonna deal with their accusations.

Break out the champagne. We could party forever after stress and trauma by the unclever and the pain.

Think of what they put us through! Not only these criminals but their fans: the liberals were so cruel!

Please help us Father to banish the brutish child rapist--the smelly hippy monster, so foolish and ruthless.

Voter Decoder: HRC is the lowest of the low, total scum, gruesome depravity--child rape and murder.

Liberals are filthy pigs: the stuff they condone is crass, gross, sickening and negative--they're the dregs.

FRENEMY ENABLER

Why did you call me bad but condoned these awful things while wearing a smile yet filled with guile?

Being liberal was the style so you went along with out God to keep you on the right side of the aisle.

THE MAINSTREAM IS FAKE NEWS: SEEK TRUTH

The mainstream news is fake news. But the criminals in power define the truth as "alt right" views.

They control reality, run corpses for offices, run fake polls and instigate violence--and we're lawless?

Glenn Beck is now the horrible little apologist for "right wing demons". Shut up traitor, you've been beaten.

Women were respected/protected as the weaker sex but now men don't know how to act: will it make her mad?

Trump shouldn't "reach across the aisle". We don't join with commie pigs who make elections rigged.

Can't wait for local schools to take over. Until then it's pure brainwashing against Trump, our savior.

Vicious dems are now out to destroy Pence the same as Flynn.

The next 3 months will be the most profitable in U.S. corporate history.

The truth of Donald Trump of course draws protestors more than us busy/successful deplorables.

Always an ace in the hole I believe. So many faces of adaptation and shrewd tricks up his sleeve.

The greatest country in the history of civilization--America--she said she hated (Arianda).

Letting em off easy is the soft bigotry of lowered expectations.

FRENEMY ENABLER

Mental warzone cannot be bridged--they're too dumb to think deeply/get angry when challenged.

There is a great Determiner who decides the fate of nations.

Germany is: conformity. Americana is: individuality. And that's why they're sunk and we're free.

LIBERALISM: OPEN BORDERS TO FOES

Liberalism: Open borders to those wanting to kill us, take our guns and teach our kids filthiness.

Open borders to foes, kill offspring, sexualize kids, take away self-defense: liberalism is a mental illness.

It's a giant temper tantrum that they lost on all levels--they wanna blow the whole world up, the devils.

Once you see how liberalism is a mental illness it changes your reaction to the clowns and their silliness.

Affluent liberals and the red carpet: a reflection of emptiness and soullessness that makes the clear hate it.

The TV's red carpet (rich liberal crap) makes them like gods and you small, but none of it means a thing at all.

In 1920 they merged Hollywood with politicians who "looked good". We've been stuck in this falsehood.

Though they lost they keep fighting. If they don't quit, massive more leaks will come out and they'll submit.

Obama pushed 25 million people out of the middle class---an extraordinary negative achievement. Newt Gingrich

It won't work cuz Trump has charisma and brains. Not riding a media horse into the White House then ill fame.

FRENEMY ENABLER

Not surrounding himself with a bunch of academics like Obama, but guys with intelligence and street smarts: eureka!

Democrats are the Politics of Division.

They may start a nuclear war in a temper tantrum like toddlers to stop humanity in it's epic progress.

Obama's true legacy is the destruction of the democrat party. Michael Savage

They hate Trump to be part of the clique. They don't know anything at all: same old crap, they're thick.

Though well-funded it'll reach a point where anti--Trumps are isolated into one lump, discredited as dumb.

Knew before Donald Trump became president of the greatest republic the world's ever seen, we're rid of fiends.

Stealing farmers/ranchers property under environmental garbage, sending evil messages and creating carnage.

Understand: We need Putin (for terrorism/plans) and he's become a smart man. Liberals want war--scam!

FOX MAKES DISTINCTIONS WITHOUT DIFFERENCES

FOX making distinctions without differences, taking up all the time saying nothing--that's my two cents.

Don't take Paul Ryan along for the ride, oust him from the house! Remember the spending bill Omnibus?

So, Putin made a fool out of him on the world stage so now he's gonna stick it to him in a rage.

After undermining everything this country stands for he wants to block Trump to make her great/prosper?

Obama's Cold War Deja-Vu: "hapless"

FRENEMY ENABLER

Obama's goal destroying America shown in the wrench he was throwin but God was watching/He's our champion.

Russians: "the unpredictable/aggressive Obama foreign policy" means: burn down house before he leaves.

This isn't like stealing the furniture, this is dangerous.

What cost Hillary the presidency was the fact she's a crook with out a personality.

AMERICA IS LIBERTY PRINCIPALS: HARDLY EVIL!

They put America down as evil--but who's there in a disaster, people?

Kitchen Diplomacy: like a husband and wife arguing in the kitchen.

He's mad at Americans for kicking the bums out--900 state seats--so he's gonna do us all in, not just pout.

Make it new, go for it. Play the Trump card, it's there for you to take--he proved the only block is yourself. Gerald Celente

Dems lost one thousand seats, but he woulda won?

Good riddance Megyn Kelly, won't see your face again cuz it's been creepy, scary, petty.

Black Lives Matter has become ISIS torturers. But look who both were created by: politicians/lecherers.

Deplorable: You call us names and we'll wear the name proudly and run right over you. Newt Gingrich

Democrats just never give up: If at first you don't succeed, cry cry again.

Ben Carson rose from poverty to become a world class surgeon and they said "he can't figure out Hud".

They're really good at taking tests/writing essays getting them into first class colleges: intellectual idiots.

FRENEMY ENABLER

Obama will be sober by summer watching everything he thought he accomplished go away. Newt Gingrich

How can we ever trust the media again, after they went for Hillary Clinton?

So sick of hearing tired cliches: xenophobic, homophobic, sexist, bigot, racist, Islamophobic/shove it.

If lucky we'll be rid of leftists, liberals, progressives, RINOS and neo-cons: targeted and gone.

DEMOCRATS LOVE HOLLYWOOD ELITES

Democrats love Hollywood elites not the common man or police.

Through Obama the American Dream was ripped out of our guts. Hannity

My indictments against Obama are actually directed towards the whole leftist scene, still in control and mean.

They're making millions on youtube with nothing to say. Amazing.

Way of Obama: Give positions to those knowing nothing about it.

Liberalism was a terrible dark cloud imposing on us for 50 years.

We're so gleeful with President Trump and he hit the ground running! Oh boy, just wait--he's SO cunning.

American Revolution started when they came to take the guns. Learn from that/tell your grandsons.

Obama is literally less popular than the crackhead mayor of Toronto now. Not a good thing, but wow!

All crises are used by governments everywhere to increase their power, for sure--so listen, watch: mature.

The answer to 1984 is 1776. Alex Jones

FRENEMY ENABLER

What if when Obama won a republican said those things against him--would've been cataclysmic/bad sin.

Cheer up America, your greatest days are ahead of you--as God raises up an army to fight for you.

The nature of power: it concentrates more power unto itself. Let in low-wage workers and to citizens: farewell.

Stay away from non-believers. For what business/why revere? Stay clear-- have no dinner even a beer.

Trading liberty for security won't make you safe--it'll just make you dependent, controlled and a slave.

Logic, common sense and reason: We're coming into a great season so ignore the Hollywood scum for their treason.

Having abandoned God, liberalism is their religion and that's why losing it is apostasy to them: treason, enablin'.

100 KAREN KELLOCK BOOKS

AFFINITY OR MISERY
AGELESS CORNUCOPIA
AMERICA AWAKE!
AMERICA'S DAFT ERA
ARTS OF PALEO FASTING
AUTOPHAGY ON CHEATERS
BACKSTABBING NEUROTICS
BETRAYAL TRAUMA
BOOMERS AND BROKENNESS
BOOT ON NECK
CHAMPION GUIDES
COMMIE NUTHOUSE
COMMIES
COMMUNIST SPIRIT
CONTAGION OF MADNESS
CONTAGIOUS MADNESS
CULTURE CLASH BASHED
DAFT LEFT
DAILY FASTARIAN
DAM RATS
DIVERSITY IS CRUELTY
E-RACE WHITE
EVIL FREAKS (Beyond Gross)
THE END OR A BEND?
FEMALE BULLIES AND FEMI-NAZIS
FEMALE CARNALITY
FEMALE DUMB DOWN
FEMALE POWER DRIVE
FEMINISM AND RUIN 1 & 2
FIX FOR MISFITS
FOOLS & TRAMPS
FREEDOM SPEAKING
FRENEMY ENABLER
FRENEMY LIAR
FRENEMY THIEF
FRENEMY TRAITOR
TRENEMY TYRANT
GENIUS IS HELD DOWN
GLOBALISLAM
GOD USES THE FLAWED
HAZE OF THE LATTER DAYS

THE HERD IN WORDS
HIX POLITIX
HOW THEY RUINED US
JUST SKIP DINNER
LE FEMME AND THE COMMUNIST SPIRIT
LIBERAL CHAOS & ROT
LIBERAL DOUBLETHINK
LIBERAL GALL 1 & 2
LIBERAL SHOVE-DOWNS
LOCK YOUR GATE
LOSERS and Femme Fatales
MANUAL FOR SUPERIOR MEN
MODERN ART FROM HELL
MOSTLY FAKE
NOTES TO CHAMPS 1 & 2
OVERCOME FRENEMIES
PC MAKES US CRAZY
PEOPLE ARE CRUEL
PEOPLE PROBLEMS 1 & 2
PERSECUTED GENIUIS
POLI-PSYCH MYSTERIES
PRETENTIOUS SLOBS
QUEEN BEE
RED NEW DEAL
RETURNING TO FIRST NATURE
SEASON OF TREASON
SEPARATE MEANS HOLY
SOCIAL HYPNOTISM
SOLITUDE SOLUTION
SUPERCILIOUS
THE SCHOOLS SCREWED EM UP
TOAD TO PRINCE
TRIALS CYCLES
TRUMP VS. GROUP
TRUST IN TRASH
THE TRUTH ABOUT PEOPLE
UNDERHEANDEDLY CLEVER
WALK TALL WITHIN WALLS
WE'RE NOT ALL ONE
WINNERS SKIP DINNER
WORK OR SMERK

AUTHOR BIO

Karen Kellock Ph.D.

Ph.D Political Psychology, UCI 1976
Post-Doctoral: UCI Medical School
Department of Psychiatry
Grants NIMH, NIAAA

Ph.D. dissertation "A Systems-Theoretic View of Pathologic Interaction" made an early mark as the "Wife of the Alcoholic Syndrome". Postdoctoral research at UCI Medical, Dept. of Psychiatry on the systems surrounding pathology on NIMH and NIAAA federal grants: *The Contagion of Madness: The Psychology of Neurotic Interaction and Pathological Systems*. Therapy tool Therapeutic Playwriting introduced the play *Mary and Murv: Gruesome Twosomes in the Alcoholic Marriage*. She taught Abnormal Psychology and Pathological Systems Theory at UC and CSU campuses and developed "the Debris Theory of Disease" in five books and website: (www.karenkellock.org): *Champion Guides, Daily Fastarian, Just Skip Dinner, Arts of Paleo Fasting, Ageless Cornucopia. Manual for Superior Men is a* pick-it-up-anywhere book that you can't put down (20,000 Kellockialisms) and ever on your desktop it should be found (or this Ebook for superior wordsearch of new jargon).